199 ideas

Build a Better Board

EDITED BY **DOUGLAS M. KLEINE, CAE**

PUBLISHED BY
ASAE: THE CENTER FOR ASSOCIATION LEADERSHIP

★ **asae**
The Center for Association Leadership

WASHINGTON, DC

The contributors have worked diligently to ensure that all information in this book is accurate as of the time of publication and consistent with standards of good practice in the general management community. As research and practice advance, however, standards may change. For this reason it is recommended that readers evaluate the applicability of any recommendations in light of particular situations and changing standards.

ASAE: The Center for Association Leadership
1575 I Street, NW
Washington, DC 20005-1103
Phone: (202) 626-2723; (888) 950-2723 outside the metropolitan Washington, DC area
Fax: (202) 220-6439
Email: books@asaecenter.org
We connect great ideas and great people to inspire leadership and achievement in the association community.

Keith C. Skillman, CAE, Vice President, Publications, ASAE: The Center for Association Leadership
Baron Williams, CAE, Director of Book Publishing, ASAE: The Center for Association Leadership

Cover design by Beth Lower, Art Director, ASAE: The Center for Association Leadership and Troy Scott Parker, Cimarron Design
Interior design by Troy Scott Parker, Cimarron Design

This book is available at a special discount when ordered in bulk quantities. For information, contact the ASAE Member Service Center at (202) 371-0940.

A complete catalog of titles is available on the ASAE: The Center for Association Leadership website at www.asaecenter.org.

ISBN-13: 978-0-88034-332-9
ISBN-10: 0-88034-332-X

Copyright © 2011 by ASAE: The Center for Association Leadership.

All rights reserved. Permission to reproduce or transmit in any form or by any means, electronic or mechanical, including photocopying and recording, or by an information storage and retrieval system any portion of this work must be obtained in writing from the director of book publishing at the address or fax number above.

Printed in the United States of America.

10 9 8 7 6 5 4 3 2 1

CONTENTS

Introduction and Acknowledgments v

Recruiting Board Members 1

Providing Effective Orientation 9

Communicating About Finances and Fiduciary Responsibilities 15
   Finances 15
   Fiduciary Responsibilities 18

Documenting Board Activities 21

Focusing on Policy and Strategy 27

Engaging Board Members 35

Streamlining and Improving Meetings 41

Making Board Dialogue Effective 49

Ensuring Effective Board-Staff Relationships 55

Enhancing the Board Member's Experience 63

Evaluating the Board 67

Bibliography 71

Share Tips with Colleagues 75

INTRODUCTION AND ACKNOWLEDGMENTS

Conversations about association governance often center on the question, "What is the ideal board?" Opinions differ, of course. However, even if an association had the ideal board, would that be enough? Whatever the qualifications of board members, boards still need leadership, processes, priorities, and good relationships with staff to be effective. Boards also need thoughtful succession processes to maintain the perfect composition. Making sure these components are in place will help you to build a better board for your association.

To that end, this book collects 199 ideas from association executives, consultants, and others on recruitment, orientation, engagement, meeting processes, board room focus, evaluation, and more. These ideas were researched, compiled, and adapted from ASAE publications, outside sources, and from tips and insights contributed by colleagues like you. The collection does not constitute a "best practice statement." In fact, you may think that some of the ideas contradict others. We can only say that every idea worked at least once in one set of circumstances for one board. Some ideas may simply be conversation openers between elected leaders and staff along the lines of "What if we….?"

It is up to you to examine each idea in the context of your association, your board, your culture, and where your association is and would be willing to go along a continuum of hands-on boards to boards with noble thoughts and balanced scorecards. Certainly, factors such as international versus locally focused associations, frequency and length of meetings, and availability of resources to support outside help or extra retreats all bear upon whether a particular idea can make a difference for your association.

As the association management profession evolves, the job of effectively leading and governing associations grows more complex. The inherent changes often occur at a rate faster than that with which many—staff and elected leaders—are comfortable. In such a climate, it is to our advantage to be able to benefit from other colleagues' experiences. Some were on the "bleeding edge" of change, others saw simple solutions to exasperating problems, and some saw new paradigms.

We thank them all for their contributions and encourage you to continue their work by sharing your innovations, ideas, successes, and lessons learned through the many publication, education, and networking outlets available to you through ASAE. Please consider giving back to the community by sharing a tip for possible inclusion in future publications. Check out the back pages of this book, or go to **www.asaecenter.org/sharemytip**.

Our "199 Ideas" series is always growing, and we're always looking for ideas in many topic areas.

Our sincerest thanks goes to the following contributors and to all those who share their experiences through ASAE.

EXECUTIVE EDITOR

Douglas M. Kleine, CAE

PROJECT EDITOR

Apryl Motley, CAE

CONTRIBUTORS

Bridget Brown
Executive Director
National Association of Workforce Development Professionals
Washington, DC

Susan A. Cantrell
Vice President, Resources Development
American Society of Health-System Pharmacists®
Bethesda, MD

Diane James, CAE
Foundation Director & CEO
Women's Transportation Seminar Foundation
Washington DC

Carol Freysinger
Senior Consultant
Kellen Company
Washington, DC

Betty Kjellberg
Principal
Association Solutions, LLC
Scottsdale, AZ

Michael J. Nizankiewicz, CAE
Interim Executive and Affiliated Consultant
Transition Management Consulting
Washington, DC

Michele White, CAE
Director of Communications and PR
Florida Association of the American Institute of Architects
Tallahassee, FL

Patrick Winters, CAE
President and Chief Executive Officer
Strategic Evaluations and Executive Transitions, LLC
Maylene, AL

199 ideas

RECRUITING BOARD MEMBERS

1. Develop and maintain an updated, detailed, two-part profile of the desired board in terms of overall composition and the attributes and qualifications of individual board members.
Employ this profile more or less directly in systematically influencing the filling of board vacancies.

2. Build a pipeline of potential board members and leaders.
You can do this by creating an "emerging leaders" or "rising stars" group and hosting special events and training for this group. For instance, one association holds quarterly breakfast meetings for this group during which they participate in leadership development training. The goal is to prepare them to step up to committee or board positions. When you have open spots on committees or your board, look to this group to fill them.

3. Look to chapters, committees, and other components (interest groups, foundation, etc.) for potential leaders.
These are testing grounds for potential leaders and provide a glimpse of delegation, organizational, and communications skills, as well as interaction with staff. Caution: One of the biggest adjustments leaders have to make is moving from an environment with no staff, such as a local chapter, to an environment with active staff involvement.

4. Use your annual meeting to begin the recruitment process.
Hold a briefing for prospective candidates, covering the role of the board, your reimbursement policy, time requirements, and nomination and election processes and deadlines.

5. Choose committee members carefully.
A few past board members might provide insight into the requirements of the job, but also look to people who have wide networks and can reach candidates outside of the inner circle. If you want to change a board, choose a committee composed of people who reflect that future board.

6. Consider whether there is a future president or chair among the slate of candidates for board seats.
If the chief elected officer is chosen by the board, then each year's slate needs to pass the test of answering the question, "Is there someone on this slate who could be president in three years or less?"

7. Establish a year-round committee.
Because board recruitment and nominations constitute such an important activity, begin looking at the process as a year-round committee function instead of the traditional ad hoc nominations process. Reflecting this long-range focus, many boards are changing the name of their nominations committees to the board development committee because developing leaders includes more than nominating people to serve on our boards. It truly is an ongoing, year-round function: prospecting, contacting, recruiting, orienting, supporting, providing ongoing training, and evaluating board directors.

8. Link recruitment to the strategic plan.
It is important to match board recruitment and development activities with the new requirements and demands called for by the strategic plan. The ideal time to do this is right after the strategic planning process has been completed. The organization board, or the board development committee, reviews the mission, vision, goals and strategies, and then determines any new skills, knowledge, personal contacts and other attributes future board

directors will need to possess for the board to do its part in advancing the strategic plan.

9. Profile the current board.
At the same time, analyze the current shape of the organization's board. The board development committee can create a profile of the current board using a matrix designed for this purpose. Key factors that define sought-after expertise, knowledge, skills, experience, and relevant demographic factors are arranged down the side of the matrix. The names of current board directors are listed along the top of the matrix. The committee then uses the matrix to complete the profile.

10. Focus the recruiting priorities.
By reviewing the organization's strategic plan as well as the profile of current board strengths and weaknesses, the board development committee identifies the gap between the skills and knowledge needed on the board and what board directors currently possess. Based on this analysis, the board development committee can now set clear recruiting priorities for future board recruitment.

11. Develop a written board director job description.[1]
Another key element in the board development process is a written board director job description. For the organization's governance board to operate successfully, each member must understand and accept the specific duties and responsibilities that come with board directorship. More and more organizations have found it helpful to develop a written statement or agreement for board directors. The job description, in very clear language, sets forth the expectations the organization has of its board directors. The most effective job descriptions are those that state in behavioral terms precisely what board directors are expected to do.

---

[1] Ideas 7–11 reprinted with permission from "Developing a Board Recruitment Plan," <www.createthefuture.com/developing>, The Center for Public Skills Training; Frank Martinelli, President.

11 Qualifications of the Ideal Director

Every member of a board of directors is a spokesman for an entire group, industry, or profession, and as such, has the ability to enhance or denigrate its reputation. In addition, every director should be viewed as a potential chief elected officer, just as he or she was likely identified as a potential director when serving as a committee chairman or member. Committee and board meetings are an excellent screening ground.

Because of the importance of the selection process for directors, the association executive and nominating committee should use a checklist of qualifications such as the following:

1. **The potential board member must be interested in more than the honor inherent in the position.** Selection for board participation represents a serious commitment; it is not merely a reward.

2. **The candidate must be able to devote adequate time to the job.** Experience as a committee chairman or in other association service is a helpful indicator, but a commitment to give the necessary time is useful. Some associations have a written policy dictating the automatic removal of board members with a number of unexcused absences from board meetings.

3. **The board candidate should be in reasonably good health.** Does the candidate have the mental and physical energy required? Selection to the board of directors should not be seen as a tribute to someone in declining health. Many forms of recognition are available for ailing members.

4. **The perspective board member should be able to work effectively with the association chief executive.** Unique teamwork is demanded of an association chief executive and of each elected leader. Effective communication and the ability to get along well with one another are essential.

5. **The director candidate should be able to tolerate the limelight as well as the inevitable criticism of leadership.** Popularity is required to achieve leadership, but cannot be more important than an individual's judgment and integrity. An association's elected leader should be reasonably self-effacing in the spotlight and tolerant of member criticism resulting from changes within the association or new courses of action.

continued on next page

continued from previous page

6. **The prospective director should communicate effectively with other directors, with the association as a whole, and with the public.** "Great minds" who cannot communicate well with others are unlikely to make significant contributions as association board members.

7. **Personal, business, and regional biases of board candidates must be subordinated to the good of the group.** Directors are expected to reflect the special feeling of their own constituencies, but must always put the interest of the industry or profession they serve first.

8. **The candidate's personal conduct must reflect favorably upon the group and the association.** No association has a right to meddle in personal affairs, but individuals who are notorious for unorthodox behavior may prove to be more irritating or embarrassing than amusing or helpful.

9. **If the prospective director is married, his or her spouse should be supportive rather than obstructive or resentful.** An association has a right to expect a director's spouse to be understanding rather than critical of the extra demands on the spouse's time. Spouse support is enhanced when directors are encouraged to bring their spouses to board meetings.

10. **After his or her term of office, the volunteer leader should step down gracefully.** Every director cannot become chief elected officer, and even the latter's term of office is limited. Association leaders should be selected with a view to their potential continuing statesmanlike contributions after their terms have expired.

11. **A director candidate should be a proven performer.** The director should have high integrity and an understanding of the ethics of the community and of his or her calling. He or she should be knowledgeable, experienced, capable, and active—a proven performer.

Reprinted from *Principles of Association Management* edited by Henry Ernstthal, CAE, ASAE, 1988.

12. Request and review resumes, conduct interviews, and even check references to determine how closely individuals match your board's desired attributes and qualifications.

Even if your board can't directly do the screening through one of its committees, nothing prevents the board from recommending to the responsible body that such screening be done as part of the nominating process.

13. Develop a board application for prospective new board members.

The form should solicit information about the potential new member, including biographical information, why they want to join this board, what they hope to bring to the board, what they would like to get from their board membership, and any questions they might have.

14. Provide names of several board members whom the prospective new member might contact with any questions.

Potential candidates for board positions may feel more comfortable talking with a peer or colleague about any concerns they may have about serving the association in this capacity.

15. Invite the prospective board member to attend a board meeting.

Notify current board members that a potential new member will be attending. Introduce the member right away in the meeting and, at the end of the meeting, ask the potential new member if he or she has any questions.

16. Consider letting outsiders in.

Organizations with boards full of people who come from the same industry may be cultivating blind spots and groupthink. If you get a good mix of people and backgrounds and perspectives on a board you can get a much healthier organizational leadership as a result.

17. Get diverse.

As part of the nominating process, evaluate diversity. In doing so, you might take the following diversity criteria, among others, into consideration: industry segment, geographic location, membership category, ethnicity and gender of individuals, size of organizations (to ensure appropriate representation from small, medium, and large organizations), and functional expertise of individual members.

18. Make sure prospective board members know what will be expected of them before they agree to have their names included on the ballot.
Provide information to prospective nominees on board members' responsibilities, including fiduciary responsibilities, time and travel requirements, and your organization's policies on board conflicts of interest, restrictions on board members' activities, and social networking policies. Informing prospective candidates in advance will help avoid ill will and future pitfalls that may occur when board members are taken by surprise by the demands on their time or restrictions on their activities associated with their roles as elected leaders.

PROVIDING EFFECTIVE ORIENTATION

19. Start orientation with the election cycle.
Give candidates background material and make staff, the treasurer, and the chief elected officer available for questions from candidates. Using appropriate confidentiality agreements, put candidates on the distribution list for the executive director's monthly report to the board and similar communications that will give candidates a feel for the level of activity and what issues are brewing.

20. Schedule orientation sessions, either one on one or at a separate meeting, for new board members prior to their first board meeting.
Give them a packet of information on board responsibilities along with key information on the organization such as the bylaws, budget, strategic plan, board member contact information, and financials. Orientation allows new board members to become familiar with their duties and the organization's internal workings, thus enabling them to contribute from the start.

21. Provide an overview of the organization.
Incoming board members often have little experience with the organization beyond their membership experience. Board orientation manuals are helpful, even necessary, but often go unread. The CEO should review the mission statement; this will help board members see the organization more globally. Introductions by senior staff, including brief overviews of departmental responsibility, staffing, and budget, are helpful.

In the process of shaping the future of the organization, board members need to respect organization tradition and the wisdom of the previous leadership. Encourage them and help them to understand the institutional identity of the association, who the organization is, and why it operates in certain ways.

22. Ask members to discuss their goals.
Newly elected board members should be given the opportunity to express their interest in joining the board. Why are they there, what do they hope to achieve, and what expectations do they have of the leadership?

23. Define the role of the board.
Impress on new members that the board is a deliberative body, setting policy and engaging in both strategic and long-range planning. The board is not a forum for operational management. Some board members will have had prior board experience while others have had none. Many times board members have little managerial experience in their profession. Board members may try to manage instead of lead because they don't understand the difference.

At the orientation, describe the board meeting setting, who attends and who runs the meeting, how issues are identified within committees and placed on a board agenda, and so forth. The role of staff should be clear; the route to staff should be just as clear.

> **New Board Member Orientation Materials Checklist**
>
> A "New Board Member Orientation Materials Checklist" is available for ASAE members in the Models & Samples section of our website. Log in and go to **www.asaecenter.org/Resources/modelsdetail.cfm?ItemNumber=26966** to view the checklist.

24. Explore the board's limits of authority.[2]

Articles of incorporation and bylaws are not merely archive materials. The bylaws in particular are the "rules of the game," and each board member must recognize the importance of understanding and playing by these rules. Board members are granted certain authority within which their actions are authorized by the organization. As such, they need to understand the limits of their authority.

25. Be clear on finances by providing an overview of the association's financial situation.

Include information that addresses several key questions: Have there been recent cuts? Is there a critical investment in a new program? What are the five-year trends in membership, conference attendance, book sales, or other significant revenue items? Is there a financial albatross that no one can determine how to shed?

26. Explain how a new board member should go about trying to get funding for a new idea.

Present an overview of the association's budget process, including when it starts and stops and the best time for providing input.

27. Review reimbursement policies.

Outline which board member expenses will be reimbursed and the process for requesting reimbursement. Be sure board members know who to contact on staff with regard to making a purchase.

---

[2] Ideas 21–24 reprinted from "Board Orientation: Pointers for a Successful Transition" by Lou Novick, *Dollars & Cents*, September 2000.

28. Don't take too long to make your point.
An attention span is only as long as a director is willing to sit. Most content can be communicated in two to three hours. If your orientation goes beyond that, possibly you have transitioned into a planning retreat or tackled other issues. For a board wanting more in-depth training, or desiring year-round leadership development, consider adding 15-minute mini-orientation sessions at subsequent board meetings. Cover additional topics such as spokesperson training, logo usage, antitrust avoidance, insurance coverage, and so forth.

29. Broaden the focus.
Many orientations focus too much on describing the organization (i.e. meet the staff, association history, structure, and so forth) and too little on actual board responsibilities. Orientation should cover four areas, allocating a percentage of time to each category: for example, about the association (30%), board responsibilities (30%), protecting the association (15%), and strategic direction and future (25%).

30. Encourage broad attendance.
Include committee chairs, chapter officers, and future leaders. If seasoned board members balk at sitting through the session, ask them to participate by sharing their leadership experiences.

31. Enlist officers to review roles and responsibilities.
Have them review what jobs belong to the board and to the staff. You may find that the member-to-member communication is a little more effective or better received than staff-to-member.

32. Involve outgoing officers or board members in the process.
Assign them to contact incoming board members to review their duties and provide an update on activities at the [most recent] board meeting. The outgoing individual will turn over the board member/chair notebook or files to the new board member/chair at the next board meeting. During this meeting, they could complete an orientation check sheet (see sidebar) to ensure transfer of information from one volunteer to another.

33. Invite the experts.
Supplement the content delivered by staff by involving "experts," who will affirm what you have been telling the board. Your CPA can explain the need for an audit committee or why the budget is formatted to meet Generally Accepted Accounting Principles. An attorney can confirm the impact of antitrust violations. An insurance agent can describe the importance of directors and officers or meeting cancellation insurance.

34. Break the ice with stories.
An orientation that includes personal stories told by current board members about their initial miscues (i.e. forgot a tux for the banquet, flubbed an introduction of a VIP, didn't change the watch and was late to the first meeting) gives everyone a chance to talk and reduces the formality and boredom factor.

35. Create quizzes or games to encourage active participation and test knowledge of basic concepts.
For example, you could give board members a "Bylaws Pop Quiz" at least once every year. You could also develop a quiz called "Whose Responsibility Is It?" to review the distinctions between board duties and staff duties. Have the participants complete the quiz on their own. Then, facilitate a group discussion about each item.

For some items, the group may see there is no universally held belief about who is doing what. In these situations, the chief elected officer and chief staff person need to proceed carefully and in concert. For other items, discussion may lead to a common definition or understanding of particular circumstances surrounding the issue, and differences can be erased.

36. Create a timeline for the association.
Ask new and current board members to mark critical points in the association's history. The timeline may mark product launches, legislative victories, major bylaw changes, and similar events that have contributed to the association's culture or to cultural changes.

COMMUNICATING ABOUT FINANCES AND FIDUCIARY RESPONSIBILITIES

Finances

37. Determine the level of knowledge required by your board.
Depending on the type of organization you represent, the level of information that your board members need in order to uphold their fiduciary responsibility will vary. For instance, there is no sense in making sure your board understands the requirements of defined-benefit pension disclosures if you only have a 403(b) defined-contribution plan. On the other hand, every board member should know the penalties for canceling a hotel contract and the performance conditions that accompany a major grant or donation.

38. Make sure your board members understand your statement of financial position, statement of activities, and statement of cash flows and how these three statements work.

Your board members are going to need to understand the basics of these statements and how they relate to one another.

39. Keep it simple.

The reports you present to the board should be simple and paint the picture they need to see. Reports should be no more than one page; in fact, the structure of your audited statements is a good model for your internal statements. Consolidate where you can, and remember that less is more.

40. Be consistent.

Changing the format of your reports on a monthly basis will only confuse your board members. Build a visual rapport with your board through your reports so that board members become increasingly familiar with what you are presenting.

41. Make sure you include good preparatory information in the board materials that go out before the meeting.

Nonfinancial people often cannot learn financial concepts on the spot; giving them time to review concepts beforehand will make for a better learning environment.

42. When you (and/or your treasurer) are presenting to the board, use that opportunity to the fullest.

Having your treasurer just read the level of assets and the amount of the net loss does not help educate your board members. Carve out 15–20 minutes on the agenda to go over some specific accounting items. If you set a plan for covering different topics across the year, you can cover a lot. And state that plan up front: Talk about how at this board meeting you are going to discuss revenue diversification; at the next meeting, you'll tackle different types of restricted net assets; and so forth.

> **Four Questions to Ask When the Board is Talking About Finances**
>
> **"Will current-year programmatic investment of funds affect future budgets as well?"** Budgets are just one-year plans within a larger financial picture. Make sure the board understands that decisions made today may have financial impacts in the future.
>
> **"Does that really make a difference given our budget?"** Arguing over a $3,000 expense in a $35 million budget is like debating whether or not to throw a penny into a fountain. Keep them out of the weeds!
>
> **"Is that a prudent way to spend the members' money?"** Keep in mind at all times that we are dealing with the members' money and we want to make sure the programs are for them.
>
> **"What message does that send about our financial situation?"** The decisions a board makes will have ramifications throughout the staff, board, and general membership. Showing financial statements with a large gain and then announcing that we are raising membership dues may send mixed messages.
>
> Reprinted from "How to Turn a Financially Clueless Board Member Into a Financial Whiz" by Rob Batarla, *Associations Now*, March 2009.

43. Treat your board members to an industry expert or a consultant once in a while.

Regularly bringing in your investment adviser or your auditor will help solidify the concepts you have been relaying. Also, it helps underscore to your board members that finance is important.

However, you should spend time with your industry expert in advance so that he or she does not go over your board members' heads. You will also want to make sure that you and your expert are on the same page. The last thing you need is to have the "utmost expert" come in and tell your board something different than what you've been saying for years.

44. Make it relatable.

Once you have identified what you want your board members to know and have begun the process of educating them, relate it to what they are already comfortable with. If your board members are government employees, talk to them about how your restricted funds are sort of like "special revenue funds." If your board members are corporate businesspeople, talk to them about how to calculate the ROI on a new membership program. If your financial information cannot be related well to your decision makers, they won't be able to make quality decisions.

45. When in doubt, the common denominator is the good old checking account.[3]
You can probably assume that your board members have a personal checking account, a mortgage, and so forth, and understand the ins and outs of their own money. Bringing the discussion down to that level isn't a bad thing: It can be a great place to start for the financially challenged board member. But it's your job to bring them up from there.

Fiduciary Responsibilities

46. Review the basics of fiduciary duties.
Every board member should understand the four main legal principles that encompass their fiduciary duties: 1) duty to act in the best interests of the organization, 2) duty to disclose other interests and avoid conflicts, 3) duty to maintain the organization's information in confidence, and 4) duty to respect corporate opportunities. See sidebar "Director and Officer Duties."

47. Make it easy for board members to identify and ask questions about financial highlights.
Be mindful about not placing too many numbers on the page. Board members should be able to get a quick feel for what's going on. Help them to stay out of the weeds and look at the big picture by highlighting key areas: growth over the last year in gross revenue, monitoring of expenses to maintain the budgeted bottom line, investment gains or losses, and trends or future implications.

---

[3] Ideas 39–45 reprinted from "How to Turn a Financially Clueless Board Member Into a Financial Whiz" by Rob Batarla, *Associations Now,* March 2009.

48. Review your financial controls.
Demonstrate to board members that the proper policies are in place to ensure that financial transactions and financial statements are being done correctly. Discuss these policies and address any questions about them.

Director and Officer Duties

"Fiduciary duty" equates with loyalty and encompasses the following four main legal principles:

1. **The duty to act in the best interests of the organization.** This duty is very broad, requiring directors and officers to exercise ordinary and reasonable care in performing their duties. When acting in their capacity of serving the organization, they must put the organization's best interests ahead of any other interests.

2. **The duty to disclose other interests and avoid conflicts.** It is common for a director of a nonprofit organization to have other interests besides those of the organization itself. One might work in a commercial firm that does business with the nonprofit organization. One might also belong to—or be a leader in—a competing nonprofit organization or one on the opposite side of public-policy matters. The fiduciary duty of a director or officer requires disclosure of these other interests to the extent and in the manner that is requested by the nonprofit organization served.

3. **The duty to maintain the organization's information in confidence.** This applies not only to information that has been marked "confidential" but also to information that the director or officer reasonably should expect the organization to want to keep confidential. Real-estate proposals or other transactions being considered by the organization are obvious examples. The same is true for strategies or prospects for litigation involving the organization.

4. **The duty to respect corporate opportunities.** Fiduciary duty does not prohibit competition by an organization's directors or officers with the organization itself. Those individuals may generally engage in the same areas of endeavor as the organization, provided such engagement causes no unfair injury to the organization.

Excerpted from "Board Member Legal Responsibilities" by Jerald A. Jacobs, *Associations Now/The Volunteer Leadership Issue*, January 2010.

49. Highlight the importance of the financial plan in relation to the strategic plan.

Emphasize that the approval of the financial plan should be taken just as seriously as the development of the strategic plan. For example, give board members specific examples of the budget being consistent with strategic and operational planning. Be sure the budget addresses how current outlays will affect future outlays and highlight these areas for board members.

50. Develop and maintain a well-constructed investment policy statement.

When developed thoughtfully, and communicated to all relevant parties, the investment policy statement goes a long way toward managing investment risk and avoiding investment disasters long before they creep up. Focus the board's attention on determining two of the most important parts of the investment policy: your risk tolerance and, based on that, your asset-allocation strategy.

DOCUMENTING BOARD ACTIVITIES

51. Be cautious and precise in preparing minutes.

Accurate minutes should be kept for all official meetings. Minutes should be a record of what was considered and accomplished at a meeting, not a record of conversations, reports, and work assignments. They should not include sidebar conversations, if they occur. Minutes serve to show what actions the board (or other group) took or did not take and help shield the organization from liability.

52. Take additional steps to document the board's exercise of its fiduciary duty.

Critical decisions of the board of directors which involve potential legal liabilities for the association or board should be given particular attention when the minutes are drafted and approved. The board has an opportunity through the minutes to carefully record its exercise of fiduciary duty.

For instance, a resolution of the board of directors can specifically record the inquiry made by the board, the findings received, the qualification of the consultants contacted, the board's reliance on the consultant's advice and recommendations and consideration for and against the actions that were evaluated by the directors. The resolution acts as a road map to document the board's compliance with the business judgment rule.

53. Don't delay or short-cut review.
Establish a standard for how soon after meetings the draft minutes should be prepared and circulated to board members. Prompt consideration of the minutes by board members and other participants will ensure that the meeting remains fresh in everyone's mind and will minimize potential uncertainty over what occurred. Explain to directors regularly how essential careful review of draft minutes is to their fiduciary obligations and to avoiding liability. Review of minutes must not be a last-minute, perfunctory process.

54. Send a copy of approved minutes to your auditor.
Your auditor will need copies at the end of the year, so this will save digging minutes out and copying them before the visit. Also it will keep your auditor current on changes in activities as well as new policies that may affect the auditor's footnotes.

55. Recognize that minute taking is a position of power.
Often it is seen as grunt work below the dignity of an officer to do. When it is suggested that staff take minutes, the executive director tries to run and hide. The board and staff should see the function as one that has important interpretative power and therefore should be handled at a high level.

56. Highlight actions taken.
Bold face motions in the minutes. Put a list of motions passed in the front of the minutes as well as including the motions at the appropriate spot in the body of the minutes.

57. Coach the chair to recap motions before they have been approved.
For example, the chair could ask the secretary who will carry out the motion, whether there is a deadline associated with it, and how accomplishment of the action will be reported back to the board.

More on Minutes

There are many opinions about how to take meeting minutes. Here are some generally accepted effective best practices.

- Minutes should indicate the place, date, and time of the meeting and the names of all participants at the meeting, including individuals arriving late or leaving early, guests, and staff.
- Include a statement in the minutes about distribution of financial reports and approval or corrections to prior minutes.
- From time to time, minutes may contain self-serving statements to protect the organization. For example: "An antitrust avoidance statement was read and distributed to the board." This is to the advantage of the organization.
- Don't have one word more than what is absolutely necessary, but do recognize that what is necessary includes some artfully drafted evidence that a board is meeting its fiduciary duties and is complying with tax and legal requirements.
- Do not retain drafts of minutes, notes, and audio or video recordings in the organization's files once the minutes are approved. The chief elected officer and staff must be sure they are discarded. The organization should have a policy about who may create audio and video recordings.
- Ask legal counsel to review minutes before they are distributed to be certain no liability is created for the association.

Sources: "Minutes Are to Protect the Organization" by Robert Harris, CAE; "The Substance of Meeting Minutes" by James A. Woehlke, Esq., CAE, *Associations Now*, February 2006.

58. Create an action matrix from the minutes.

List the motion, the person or group that has primary responsibility, and any time frames triggered by the motion. Create versions of the matrix in order by date due and in order by name of the responsible parties.

Ten Documents No Board Should Be Without

To help your board members become focused and productive, make sure they have the following information on hand. Some of it may be a standard part of your board manual; the other materials can be distributed as they become available.

1. **Strategic plans and operating budgets** illuminate the association's vision and mission for the long and short term. These documents should outline measurable goals, work in harmony with one another, and point toward rational, achievable outcomes.
2. **Bylaws** direct the way your members want their association to operate, the authority they extend to the leadership, and the responsibilities they assign.
3. **Board policies** reflect the directors' accumulated wisdom, their values, and how they wish to approach a range of issues. Being familiar with policies helps avoid plowing old ground.
4. **Committee guidelines** define each advisory group's charge; to whom or to which group the committee reports; its budget and intended composition (if any); and the tenure of its members.
5. **Board minutes** focus on action the group has taken and preempt ill-informed and distracting questions on intent and objectives.
6. **Authority annotations** clarify who among the directors, chief elected officer, and chief staff executive is expected to do what. Ideally, spell out the expectations (such as in a matrix) to be approved by the board.
7. **Volunteer leader descriptions and any contract summaries** help directors keep prerogatives in perspective.
8. **Organizational charts** clarify authority and reporting relationships.
9. **Member surveys or analyses** shed light on constituents' wants, needs, and expectations.
10. **Program and project analyses** summarize objectives, assumptions, budgets, benchmarks, number of members to be served, dates, and the like.

By Gerard F. Hurley, CAE. Reprinted from *Association Management*, January 2000.

59. Create an expectation that the policy manual is always up to date.

In many associations, the policy manual goes years without updating. The secretary or the staff member responsible for keeping up the manual should update it after each meeting based on actions at that meeting, and redistribute it to the board and staff.

TIP: If this is burdensome, you may be classifying minor things as policy, or you may be reversing policy too frequently.

60. Use minutes to highlight information members need to know.

Look at each set of minutes to make a judgment of what should be reported in the next newsletter or magazine and what should go into a file of material for the annual report.

61. Consider a modified dashboard for reporting board actions to your members.

Without giving away trade secrets, this kind of communication can keep boards focused on making progress. It can also be a test for any board meeting, by asking, "Have we done anything yet that is worth communicating to members?"

62. Review the parking lot.

It is likely that not all parking lot issues will be dealt with at the meeting. Review the issues with the chair after the meeting, agree on how to handle each issue, and communicate with the interested board member.

63. Be consistent.

Once you establish guidelines for preparing board documents, stick to them. Board members or other reviewers should be able reference information easily because they know where to look for it.

64. Write well and edit.

Principles of good drafting applicable to contracts or other legal writing also apply to drafting minutes. Use concise, unambiguous language to avoid having a court look to other sources for clarification, explanation, or definition. Take care to ensure that the minutes are accurate and complete, consistent in language and approach and free from unnecessary information or potential traps.

Carefully review and edit the minutes to eradicate mistakes (such as indicating the presence of an absent director or vice versa) that call the entire record into question. Strive to use language that is as neutral as possible, and stay away from adjectives or adverbs reflecting your own value judgments. Avoid confusion by using "standard English" (all words used in their ordinary and normal sense.)

199 ideas

FOCUSING ON POLICY AND STRATEGY

65. Write the annual report before the year starts.
Not literally, but have a conversation with the chief elected officer about what some of the headlines would be. Go over the list again before setting the agenda for each meeting.

66. Be realistic about where your board is on the continuum from operational management to strategic thinking and action.
If the typical board agenda is full of operational items and committee reports, and the meeting ends with a lot of leftover items, it will take a joint effort between the board and staff to move to strategy, and the effort will likely be gradual.

67. In moving to strategy, prepare the board for "giving up" traditional areas of involvement.
At some point, there must be a zero-sum reallocation of time and energy from operations to strategy. If the board is used to detailed involvement in conferences, awards, and legislative tactics, the move to strategy can create a feeling of being set adrift at sea until there is clear articulation of strategic direction and policy. Letting go will

be easier if you can create a high degree of confidence in staff's or a committee's ability to carry out operations that used to consume board time.

68. Create an agenda that ensures that strategic visioning and policy development are the primary focus.

Put big picture items on the agenda at times when the board is fresh, such as at the front of the agenda on day 1, or if your meeting starts in the afternoon, as the first item on day 2, so that they don't get relegated to a rushed discussion or tabled until the next meeting, and they are not discussed when everyone is tired.

69. Encourage the board to use its informed intuition in decision-making by providing board members with the knowledge they need to decide what happens next for the association.

Successful governance uses informed intuition, which can be a source of insight of equal importance to hard data about current conditions or past performance. As Glenn H. Tecker et al. outline in *The Will to Govern Well*, informed intuition occurs at the confluence of what the board learns about four knowledge bases: (a) member wants, needs, and preferences; (b) external marketplace dynamics and realities; (c) capacity and strategic position of the organization; and (d) ethical implications of its choices. To have confidence in and understanding of any significant decision, the governing body needs insight into the four knowledge bases relative to any issue. This approach represents a new balance between being politically correct and being appropriately and sufficiently knowledgeable.

70. Make sure your strategic-planning process involves soliciting input from the board throughout the process.

It's very disheartening to board members if they are only involved in the process on the tail-end. They want to do more than page through the document that staff members have created, and you should want that as well.

> **Markers of Strategic Boards**
> - Focus their meetings on governing rather than managing.
> - Help shape the organization's priorities through the strategic planning process.
> - Align agendas with goals and priorities.
> - Place high priority on addressing long-range strategic issues that confront the organization.
> - Anticipate potential problems before the issues become urgent.
> - Sharpen direction, address difficult issues, and identify opportunities.
> - Allocate time to what matters most to the performance and success of the organization.
>
> Reprinted from *Governing For Growth: Using 7 Measures of Success to Strengthen Board Dialogue and Decision Making* by Nancy Axelrod, ASAE, 2009.

71. Relate action items on your meeting agendas to the strategic plan.

Requests for board action from committees, staff, and others should reference the section of the strategic plan that is related to the request and its hoped-for result.

72. Appoint a plan monitor.

Put a respected volunteer leader in a position to monitor and report on progress and impediments in implementing the strategic plan. The status report should be on the consent agenda only if everything is going according to schedule. Otherwise, talk about it.

73. Nourish a champion.

It's much better if the torch is carried by a board member than by the CEO. Supporting a champion for better governance allows the CEO to be as helpful as he or she wishes without compromising the board's role as employer. Rather than manipulating the board, the CEO is encouraging a board member in his or her mission.

74. Capitalize on retreat opportunities.
Because boards often leave retreat planning to their CEO, he or she can use that opportunity to schedule a thorough examination of the governance process that would propel the board into a new level of understanding of its job. Paradoxically, if such an event is successful, the board would never leave retreat subject matter to the CEO again but would assume responsibility for its own improvement.

75. Furnish reading material.
CEOs are in an excellent position to supply governance-related reading materials to their boards. In addition to articles and monographs, CEOs can buy books for board members who, after all, get precious few perks in their volunteer role.

76. Don't invite the board to manage.
In numerous ways, CEOs actually encourage board intrusions into managerial issues. For example, asking selected, qualified individuals for advice causes no problem, but asking the board as a body for advice does. In addition, bringing detailed managerial reports to the board turns board meetings into management meetings.

77. Assume as-if policies.[4]
In the absence of clear board policies, a CEO can make it a priority to tell the board that he or she is managing as if the board has a policy that says "X" (fill in the blank). This isn't nearly as good as the board's creating its own policies, but it does protect the CEO until the time the board catches on and sees to its own job. Given a little luck, the board will alter the CEO's version and create wording of its own.

78. Concentrate on long-term outcomes.
The board's role is to think long-term and to ensure that the organization has the discipline to think long-term by writing broadly defined policies to ensure that a picture of the organization's

---

[4] Ideas 73–77 reprinted from "Reinventing Governance" by John Carver, *Association Management*, August 1999.

long-term outcomes is defined. These outcomes are beyond goals and strategy. They have to do with why and how the organization justifies its existence. These policies support the organization in its long-range planning processes.

79. Set up a "dashboard."
A dashboard is a visual summary of carefully selected performance measures that allow board members to see, at a glance, the status of an association's progress on its most important priorities.

Tips for Setting Up a Dashboard

80. Involve the board in defining which metrics to include so they own it.
Also involve key staff to ensure implementation is doable.

81. Focus on mission imperatives and drivers of strategy.
"Dashboards should be a top-level, high-level view of things that speak to overall performance," says Lawrence Butler, senior consultant of Maguire Associates and author of *The Nonprofit Dashboard: A Tool for Tracking Progress* (BoardSource, 2007).

82. Provide context where possible.
How does a particular statistic compare to the budget, to stated goals, to other associations, or to last year?

83. Keep the format clean, uncluttered, and consistent.
If they see it in the same arrangement and format from meeting to meeting, they can quickly spot changes and patterns.

84. Include a column for "warning signals," such as a red dot for metrics not meeting preset goals.
When trouble spots appear, evaluate the metric as well as what it was set up to measure.

85. Be clear about the role of a dashboard.[5]
It is primarily a barometer for course correction; using it to evaluate the performance of key staff is ancillary. These should be used to make policy decisions, not to be micromanaging.

86. Tie the chief staff officer's performance objectives to the strategic plan.
While there may be other things you want to address in the coming year, there should be no more important accomplishment than meeting the objectives that have been mutually agreed upon by you and the board.

87. Take organizational culture into account when making policy and strategy decisions.
Be very clear about your organizational culture and articulate the unwritten rules. Numbers and logic may point you in one direction, but if that is counter to what your association values, listen to the organizational gut.

88. Establish clarity of purpose around strategic discussions.
Ask two questions: Why are we scheduling this discussion? What is the overall objective? Whether it is to generate ideas, gather facts, or learn what is not known, the purpose of the discussion should be clear.

For example, are board members being asked to participate in this strategic thinking discussion to be informed about strengths, weaknesses, opportunities, and threat? Or is the purpose to expose the board to best practices or trends in the field? Is the objective to invite the board to brainstorm about what is known about drivers of change and to provide guidance on identifying what is not known?

Perhaps the purpose is for the board to deliberate on the pros and cons of potential outcomes for an embryonic issue or an ambiguous threat. Yet another objective might be to get a sense of the board

---

[5] Ideas 82–85 adapted and reprinted from "The Right Metrics for Association Boards" by Whitney Redding, *Associations Now/Volunteer Leadership Issue*, January 2010.

well before action is required or a decision from the board must be made on an action step to move forward.

> **Successful Strategic Thinking Discussions**
>
> What constitutes success for strategic thinking discussions will depend on their purpose. However, there are some markers of success:
>
> - The strategic discussion led to a better understanding on the board's part of the external circumstances and internal realities that drive performance.
> - Board members willing to learn from information gathered internally and externally.
> - All board members encouraged to participate in the discussion.
> - Board members put the interests of the organization above all else.
> - The board was willing to spend time exploring the alternatives and consequences of different options.
> - If consensus was needed to move to the next steps, it was reached in a fair and inclusive manner.
> - The results of the meeting clearly stated who was responsible for the implementation or next steps (e.g., staff, a board committee, an association committee, a new task force).
>
> Adapted from *Governing for Growth Facilitator's Guide* by Nancy Axelrod, ASAE, 2010.

89. Ask questions that help the board provide oversight and ensure a strategic approach.

While individual board members may be asked to provide support in implementing tasks related to strategic objectives, staff members are delegated the primary responsibility of executing policies that carry out the strategic direction of the association. The collective board can add the greatest value by addressing strategic questions such as the following:

- What could we do better in this area?
- What are the emerging new trends, best practices, or new opportunities that we should consider that could enhance our capacity?

- What metrics will best measure progress in strengthening our performance in this area?
- What resources might be needed to improve our capacity to deliver?
- What impediments are most likely to hamper our progress?
- How can the board add the greatest value in enhancing our organization's performance in this area?

90. Pose generative questions that invite the board to think creatively and expansively.[6]

- What three adjectives best describe the organization's performance in this area?
- What is the biggest gap between what we claim our performance in this area to be and what it actually is?
- What do we know about the changes in the profession or industry we serve that will have the greatest impact on our performance in this area?
- What other external trends and drivers of change will most affect our capacity to provide high-quality performance in this area during the next five years?
- What do we know about our association's capacity to tackle these issues?
- What don't we know that could improve our capacity to improve our performance in this area?
- Are there any changes that may require adjustments in the priorities or performance targets related to this area in our strategic plan?

---

[6] Ideas 86–90 adapted from *Governing for Growth Facilitator's Guide* by Nancy Axelrod, ASAE, 2010.

ENGAGING BOARD MEMBERS

91. Be open in your agenda setting process.
All board members should know how things get on the agenda and the deadline for issues to come forward as agenda items.

92. Use open space technology and have the board propose its own agenda of issues to discuss.
Using open space technology, the larger group breaks up into smaller groups that are self-selected. Their meetings will consist primarily of small group discussions. While the groups may not come back with action recommendations, the summary of their discussions could speed up action on sticky topics at future board meetings. That way everyone has the opportunity to propose topics and attend discussions that interest them.

93. Focus the agenda on results.
Look for ways to structure real discussions among board members that will elicit commitment and leadership. Decide what is needed most out of this meeting, set your agenda accordingly, and tell your board members at the beginning of the session why they are present and what you need out of them: "By the end of this meeting, we need to accomplish x, y, and z." That will get their attention.

94. Be creative with the agenda.
Look for ways to tweak the meeting plan to evoke your board members' passion for your cause. Avoid a dry recital of figures, and instead humanize your discussions by giving the board insight to what the organization is really accomplishing out in the world.

95. For a more radical approach, occasionally throw out the agenda altogether!
Let the board create its own order of business by consensus at the beginning of the meeting. That way everyone is immediately paying more attention to the work that needs to get accomplished in the meeting. They are not just meeting for routine reporting and discussing; action needs to be taken on real issues now.

96. Focus on problems, challenges, or broad issues.
Discussions of this nature will activate your board members' various backgrounds and skills sets, not to mention their interest. It will allow you to draw upon a deeper reservoir of their talent and energy and will give them more interesting work.

97. Look at trends within routine reports.
Identify larger, big-picture issues that are reflected within routine reports. For example, along with the financial report, consider a discussion of long-run implications of certain revenue or cost trends. What are three important questions anyone might want to ask about this month's financial report? Identify these questions yourself and introduce them to the board as discussion topics.

98. Plan big.[7]
Bring big-picture strategic planning issues into regular board meetings. For example, you could take the standard strategic planning issues focusing on organizational strengths, weaknesses, opportunities, and threats (SWOT analysis). Divide the four subjects over four board meetings and at each meeting, take your board through a discussion or update of one of these issues.

---

[7] Ideas 93–98 reprinted from "12 Ways to Liven up Your Board Meetings and Your Board" by Gail Perry (www.gailperry.com), Executive IdeaLink, February 2010.

99. Consider alternative room set-ups.
One association board found that it was much more comfortable with a table arranged as a long O (using curved banquet tables) rather than a hollow square or solid rectangle. Another association board meets in a circle without any table.

100. Have a star.
Bring in a guest speaker for 30 minutes who will provide information and insight that makes the whole trip worthwhile for the board: a congressional staff person, the CEO of another association, or a professor with a new study that relates to your field. These are folks whom your board members would not otherwise encounter in such an intimate environment.

101. Use icebreakers at each meeting.
This may not be as important for a local association that meets once a month in person, but for the board that comes cross country just two or three times a year, icebreakers are ways to build trust and respect. They let new members reveal more about themselves and learn more about other directors.

Engaging New Board Members

102. Schedule a personal site visit.
Invite new board members to stop in the office to meet staff, sensing the feel and passion of the organization, and having lunch with some of the key staff members. Make sure the chief staff executive is available to spend some time with them during their visit. Some chief staff executives only spend time with officers, and this is a mistake.

103. Be sure to assign the new board member to at least one committee.
This helps to engage the member in specific tasks and duties of the organization. The board member needs to realize that most of the work takes place outside of the board meetings.

104. Personalize the relationship.
Make sure you get the following information from each new board member: birthdays, anniversaries, kids' names and ages, where they work and so on, so you can acknowledge these events with a card, gift, or other tribute. Always be sure the board members know you value them as people.

105. Get commitments early.[8]
After you recruit the board members, but before the first board meeting, get commitments early in terms of what committee they will be on, how much time they will have to give to the organization, how they want their expertise and talents to be used in the organization, and what new skills they want to develop as a result of their participation on your board.

106. Summarize.
Recap accomplishments at the end of each day. Keep running minutes on a computer and project them on a screen with motions highlighted.

107. Help the group plan its dinner and pre- and post- meeting events.
Social engagement is important. Guard against cliques and invitation-only gatherings that exclude some directors.

108. Focus forward to 5, 10, or 20 years.
Engage board members in thinking about the future of the association by putting them in groups where they develop headlines (for an electronic or print publication) based on this question: "It's the year (fill in the blank). What will the headline say about our association?" Have each small group present their headlines to the larger group.

---

[8] Ideas 102–105 are from Richard Male and Associates.

109. Create a questionnaire designed to solicit the board's feedback on strategic goals.
Ask board members to comment on their perception of how goals were developed, monitored, and measured. Was the goal-setting process inclusive enough? Is it easy to determine where progress has been made towards goals and where it hasn't? These are among the questions that might be included.

110. Interview board members yearly.
Interview board members in teams of two every year to find out how the person is feeling about the organization, how much time they have to contribute, and what they want to learn and do with their time.

STREAMLINING AND IMPROVING MEETINGS

111. Provide the board book and background information well in advance of the meeting.
This will give board members ample time to review information prior to board meetings and ask questions. Accomplishing this goal is dependent upon getting materials into the office in a timely manner, which may require some help from the chair or the secretary in enforcing deadlines. Staff should set an example by providing staff reports on time.

112. What happens before the board meeting is often as important, or more important, than what occurs during it.
A good agenda, background material, and specific assignments for agenda items lead to an organized meeting and greater possibility of achieving your desired outcomes.

113. Establish etiquette by setting ground rules before the meeting begins.
Encourage the person chairing the meeting to set the tone and lead by example: "I am turning off my mobile device during this meeting, and I would like everyone else to do the same."

114. Adopt a consent agenda.

The consent agenda is a great tool for getting the non-strategic, non-controversial business items out of the way first, while simultaneously providing transparency. All the read-ahead, FYI-type items are grouped together at the beginning of the meeting, and there's a vote to accept them as a group without discussion.

If anyone wants to discuss an item, that item is removed from the consent agenda, and the remainder of the items can be voted on as a group. It creates more time in the meeting for the board to focus on big-picture, strategic issues. When the tool is used for the first

---

What to Include on Consent Agendas

Items commonly found on consent agendas include:

1. Minutes of the previous meeting
2. Confirmation of a decision that has been discussed previously
3. Chief executive's report
4. Committee reports
5. Informational materials
6. Updated organizational documents

To test whether an item should be included in the consent agenda, ask these questions:

- Is this item self-explanatory and uncontroversial?
- Does it contain an issue that warrants board discussion?
- Is this item "for information only"? Is it needed for another meeting agenda issue?
- Do we need to confirm a previously discussed issue? Do we need to continue the discussion?

Source: "The Consent Agenda: A Tool for Improving Governance," BoardSource, 2006. Reprinted with permission from www.boardsource.org. BoardSource, formerly the National Center for Nonprofit Boards, is the premier resource for practical information, tools, and training for board members and chief executives of nonprofit organizations worldwide. For more information about BoardSource, visit www.boardsource.org or call 800-883-6262. BoardSource © 2011. Text may not be reproduced without written permission from BoardSource.

time, the board chair should explain it to the group to ensure that everyone understands its purpose.

115. Use a timed agenda.
Next to each agenda item, estimate how much time it will require. This helps the chair and chief staff executive plan a realistic agenda, and all members know which items require extensive or expeditious discussion. The times are guidelines and should never prevent a board from spending enough time to seek pertinent information or engage in productive discussion.

116. Put the mission on the agenda.
At the top of every board meeting agenda, put the organization's mission and vision statements. It feels good at the meeting to see them as you work through the agenda, and everyone stays clear about them.

117. Post an acronym chart.
Make a poster of frequently used external and internal acronyms and post it on the wall of every meeting. If you distribute the list on paper it is soon lost.

118. Write an anticipated action for each agenda item.
Examples: Finance Committee report, brief questions and answers: no action needed. Volunteer recruitment and philosophy: Anticipated Action = form committee of three to four board members.

119. Avoid one-way communication from staff.
If you have a regular executive director's report on the agenda, or if a staff program director is giving you a briefing, be sure that such presentations need a response from the board. If not, put them in writing in the board book and just ask if there are any questions.

120. Don't include committee reports on the agenda just to make the committees feel worthwhile.
If a committee has done work but doesn't need it discussed, put the committee report in the board book. In the meeting, be sure to

recognize the committee's good work and refer people to the written report.

121. Adjourn on time, or agree to stay later.
Twenty minutes before the scheduled end of the meeting, the chair should ask whether the group wants to stay later: "If we continue this very interesting discussion, we will have to stay fifteen extra minutes to hear the recommendation on the executive director's salary. Can everyone stay that long, or should we end this discussion and move to that one immediately?"

122. Once every year or two, survey the board about meetings.[9]
Pass out a questionnaire for anonymous return to the board vice president or secretary. Ask board members what they like best and least about board meetings, whether they are satisfied with the items that are usually on the agenda, or how the board chair could do more to encourage discussion at the meetings.

123. Take attendance seriously.
If board members are repeatedly absent from meetings, this will affect the morale of the entire group. One option might be to amend or reinforce the provision in your association's bylaws that pertains to minimum attendance requirements (see sidebar, "Establishing Minimum Attendance Requirements.")

---

[9] Ideas 116–122 reprinted from "Ten Quick Ways to Improve Board Meetings," by Jan Masaoka in *Board Café*, 2004. This article is reprinted with permission from the *Board Café*, now part of *Blue Avocado*, a free nonprofit online magazine for community nonprofits co-sponsored by CompassPoint Nonprofit Services, Nonprofits' Insurance Alliance of California (NIAC), and Alliance of Nonprofits for Insurance, Risk Retention Group (ANI-RRG). For more information and to sign up, visit www.blueavocado.org.

Establishing Minimum Attendance Level Requirements

If your association is drafting or revising a bylaw to address attendance at board meetings, your board should build the uncertainties of life into the minimum attendance level specified by considering these points:

1. **Define attendance.** Must the director be present from convening to adjournment of the meeting or during some percentage thereof? Does telephonic attendance count? (Check to see if your state allows it.) In any case, spell out exactly what counts as attendance.

2. **Assume that perfect attendance can be expected of no one.** Then set the minimum attendance requirement at a level you think is best for the welfare of the association, irrespective of the uncertainties of life. Fix the timeframe long enough to be fair but short enough to be meaningful. For example, if the board meets quarterly and directors have three-year terms, perhaps it would be reasonable to expect attendance at a minimum of six meetings in each two-year calendar.

3. **Make the provision self-executing.** Don't require a complaint of violation to trigger the bylaw. Make it automatic. Require the secretary to monitor compliance and to file a motion in the event of noncompliance.

If this bylaw appeals to you, call your attorney, check your state's nonprofit corporation act and start talking to your board. Adopting this bylaw might make potential directors consider their duty of attendance more thoughtfully.

Excerpted from "Improving Board Meeting Attendance" by Mark Truesdell, *Associations Now,* July 2006.

Conference Call Committee Meetings

Many of your board's committees probably meet telephonically. Here are some suggestions for making sure those conference-calls are productive and run smoothly.

124. Put out a detailed agenda in advance of the call.
Because of the limitations of not meeting face-to-face, the agenda must provide much more detail to focus the discussion, even to the point of providing alternative possible decisions or courses of action. Without this focus, discussions tend to drift and one or two people tend to dominate discussion of each item.

125. Include a roster of call participants as well as those not expected on the call.
Because you do not have the visual cue of noting someone's absence, making note of committee members not on the call presents the opportunity for the chair or others to attempt to make sure the absent person's viewpoint, if it is known, is discussed. The chair has a special responsibility here.

126. Start all calls on time by taking roll.
Note who is not on the call and log them in as they join the call. Do not go back and restate the business conducted for late arrivals. This is disrespectful of those who were on time and wastes valuable time that should be spent in discussions.

127. Limit the call to no more than one hour, or two at most.
It is well documented that people's attention span drops dramatically after about 30 minutes on a phone call. You will have much more productive discussions if you schedule several one hour calls with limited agendas, than you will scheduling one long call.

128. Ask for a roll call vote on all decisions made.
Silence does not necessarily convey agreement, and without positive voting many decisions on calls do not enjoy full support after the call has ended. Make certain that everyone understands the "next steps" to be taken after each decision.

129. End the call on time.
This is critical in keeping committee members feeling positive about conference call meetings. You are much better off terminating a call on time and scheduling another call to complete the remaining business than you are keeping the call going too long.

130. Send a written report of the meeting and actions taken to the committee members immediately after the call.[10]
The dynamics of conference calls are such that people begin to remember differently both the discussions and decisions made on calls, more so than with face-to-face meetings.

131. Create a parking lot.
Keep a large sheet of paper, or an area on your whiteboard, labeled "parking lot." Before the meeting, assign one person to be in charge of the parking lot. Whenever the conversation veers off into an unforeseen (or unproductive) direction, ask board members if they would like to table the issue. If they say "yes," steer that item into your parking lot for future consideration and move forward with the agenda.

132. Touch base before the meeting.
Depending upon the size of your board, you may find it effective to call or email each board member prior to the meeting to discuss any items that might be considered either controversial or important to get approved. The result will likely be fewer surprises and shorter meetings.

133. Don't be afraid to circulate an updated agenda or additional materials.
If something important happens before the meeting but after you have circulated the meeting agenda and board package, definitely send out an update. There is no reason to save it for the meeting. Also, if a board member makes a cogent comment or agenda

---

[10] Ideas 124–130 reprinted from *Enhancing Committee Effectiveness, Revised Edition* by John F. Schlegel, PharmD, MSed, CAE; ASAE, 2009.

addition, note that and send it out. It will encourage all the other board members to be more participatory and re-focus them on the board package.

Virtual Meetings

When conducting meetings virtually, there are both opportunities and challenges. If you're interested in holding a virtual meeting, here are some things to consider before diving in, according to Harold J. Holler of the American Dietetic Association, which held its first virtual board meeting in spring 2009.

134. Allow plenty of time and preparation.
"A good six to eight months is best," says Holler. "I can't imagine getting it all done in anything less. And make sure you have enough time for training."

135. Make sure you have IT support.
"Things happen. You want to make sure you have the right people to find solutions to the problems and to keep members from getting frustrated."

136. Be realistic.
"Not all things are going to work out as planned. You may have to abandon and go with a different system. Be open to that."

137. Keep people engaged.
"We had a creative staff that was willing to step up. If they weren't engaged and excited, it would have never worked out like it did."

138. Know your participants.[11]
"If your members aren't tech savvy, don't use a tool that requires them to be so. Keep it simple; it will pay off in the end."

---

[11] Ideas 134–138 reprinted with permission from "Let's Meet Virtually, That Is" by Harold J. Holler, RD, LDN; *Associations Now/The Volunteer Leadership Issue,* January 2010.

MAKING BOARD DIALOGUE EFFECTIVE

139. Narrow the distance among board members by creating a board member yearbook.
Ask every board member to supply a detailed biographical sketch, covering both professional and personal details, and put the sketches together in a handbook distributed to all board members.

140. Rearrange the seating.
Preset name tent cards in a way that breaks up the usual seat mates and offer a different visual setting.

141. Sit the most cantankerous board member or gadfly next to the chair.
If you have more than one person that fits this description, sit them at corners. When opposing views do not have direct eye contact, views are moderated and less likely to become personal attacks.

142. Break attendees into small groups at sometime during board meetings.
Have them count off by birth date, by middle initial, by title, by the order in which they entered the room, and so forth. The greater the

variety, the better. Not only does it put different minds together, but it makes the meeting more interesting because participants never know how they will be divided.

143. Don't force the debate into pro and con.
The chair can say, "We have heard from board members for and against. Is there someone with a different view?"

144. Host an idea swap or speed brainstorming at your next board meeting.
Ask board members to move from table to table as they discuss three to five strategic issues that have been previously identified for 10–20 minutes. Designate scribes who will remain at the same table to record the ideas during each round of swapping or brainstorming. After completing the last round, have each scribe report out to the whole group on the ideas generated. Provide everyone with a written summary of the best ideas.

145. Carve out a few hours or more on the agenda for your next board meeting to discuss one or two substantive issues in a more informal conversation.
Suspend the formality of Roberts Rules of Order or other structures that inhibit spontaneous conversations. Facilitate the session so that everyone is encouraged to participate and ensure that there is space in the conversation for that to occur. You might consider engaging a skilled facilitator for the conversation.

146. Don't spend time discussing an item when you don't have enough information.
Every association board has done this at one time or another. You are faced with an issue that needs to be addressed, and you don't have adequate information available at the board meeting to fully understand or address the issue. As a result, you spend an exorbitant amount of time discussing possible scenarios that may bear no resemblance to reality, and you cover every possible "what if."

Instead of spending precious time running in circles, determine what information the board needs to fully address the issue and how you are going to obtain the information, set a deadline for obtaining the information, and place the item on the agenda for a future board meeting.

Dialogue Versus Debate

Dialogue is collaborative. Multiple sides work towards shared understanding.	Debate is oppositional. Two opposing sides try to prove each other wrong.
In dialogue, one listens to understand, to make meaning, and to find common ground.	In debate, one listens to find flaws, to spot differences, and to counter arguments.
Dialogue enlarges and possibly changes a participant's view.	Debate affirms a participant's point of view.
Dialogue reveals assumptions for reevaluation.	Debate defends assumptions as truth.
Dialogue creates an open-minded attitude, an openness to being wrong, and an openness to change.	Debate creates a close-minded attitude, a determination to be right.
In dialogue, one submits one's best thinking, expecting that the reflections of others will help improve it rather than threaten it.	In debate, one submits one's best thinking and defends it against a challenge to show that it is right.
In dialogue, one searches for the strengths in all positions.	In debate, one searches for the weaknesses in other positions.
Dialogue respects all the other participants and seeks not to alienate or offend.	Debate rebuts contrary positions and may belittle or deprecate other participants.
Dialogue assumes that many people have pieces of answers and that cooperation can lead to workable solutions.	Debate assumes a single right answer that someone already has.

Reprinted from "The Café Model: Engaging Associations in Meaningful Conversation" by Kim Porto and Janet G. McCallen, CAE (with a commentary by Jeffrey Cufaude), *Journal of Association Leadership*, Fall 2004.

147. Before the meeting, but after pre-meeting materials have been sent, encourage board members to ask for clarifying information from staff or the proponent of an action.
These pre-meeting communications can speed up deliberation at the meeting, inspire improvements to a proposal, and facilitate information sharing before discussion on its merits.

148. Use breaks to help move logjams.
Work with the chair to move breaks up or back based on whether discussion is moving at a reasonable speed. If discussion is moving quickly, then delay the break until after action has been taken so that board members can congratulate each other during the break. If discussion is bogging down, then move the break up so that hallway conversation can be used to sound out compromises.

149. Respect "firsts."
As associations reach out to a more diverse membership, many associations are getting their first Hispanic, first Muslim, first GLBT, or first overseas board member. Treat orientation as a two-way street, orienting the new board member to the board, but also leaving room for the new board member to orient the rest of the board on cultural differences and sensitivities.

150. Communicate with board members between meetings.
Creating an e-newsletter to facilitate ongoing communication between board members and staff is one option.

151. Establish a secure means for board members to communicate with one another and share resources online.
Discussion boards, board portals, and intranet sites are examples. Many organizations post board materials to dedicated, secure areas of their websites or an intranet so that their boards have easy access to any pertinent documents ranging from the strategic plan to the minutes from the last board meeting.

152. Develop a master calendar that indicates which strategic-level topic(s) will be addressed at each board and committee meeting.
Indicate what educational session(s) are needed prior to that discussion. This helps board and staff members ensure that they are fully prepared to discuss each strategic issue.

153. Engage the full board in the development of a code of conduct for board member behavior and participation in meetings.
Encourage everyone to enforce the code's guidelines during meetings and, periodically, check in at the end of board meetings on how well the guidelines are being followed.

199 ideas
ENSURING EFFECTIVE BOARD-STAFF RELATIONSHIPS

154. Cultivate a synergistic relationship.
Effective board-staff relationships start with a foundation of understanding of the primary roles of each. While in practice, the relationship is not always this black and white, the foundational principle is that the board makes policy and staff executes it. The board employs, evaluates, and sets the compensation of only one person: the chief staff executive or chief executive officer. The chief executive officer leads the staff in executing in concert with policy and strategic direction. However, as governance consultant Paul Greeley wrote in *Associations Now/The Volunteer Leadership Issue* (2008), "the lines between board and staff responsibilities are often blurred.

"While board and staff should be mindful of their primary respective roles, this interrelationship of contributions is as it should be. A thoughtful board relies on staff input for all aspects of the organization—from strategic planning to board recruitment. An enlightened staff executive welcomes the counsel of the board for areas that he or she is charged with undertaking."

155. Stay informed about what challenges your members are facing and how the association can best serve them in addressing these issues.

More than ever before, board members expect staff to be conversant with the dynamics of industrial, professional, or cause-related issues. They want staff to offer insightful, specific advice about how the association can work to meet their needs.

Board-Savvy CEOs

The board-savviest CEOs make it a point to do three things to build better relationships with their boards:

156. Bring the right attitude to the governing "business."

They welcome and celebrate strong board leadership and a close, positive, and productive partnership.

157. Make governing a top-tier priority by mastering—and devoting a healthy dollop of time to—the governing function.

They wear the "chief board developer" hat, taking accountability for helping the board build its governing capacity.

158. Pay close attention to the psychological and emotional facet of their working relationship with their boards.[12]

They come up with practical ways to provide their board members with ego satisfaction and to turn them into passionate owners of their governing work.

159. Understand how your board members prefer to communicate.

A CEO would be smart to have an open dialogue with the chair about how he or she likes to communicate—whether by phone,

---

[12] Ideas 156–158 from "The Board-Savvy CEO" in "Meeting the Governing Challenge" by Doug Eadie, *Governance Edge*, 2007.

e-mail, or in person. Find out what kinds of information your chair and board members expect to receive and then determine the best way to provide it to them.

160. Don't withhold information.
While appropriate protocols should be put in place for board members to request reports and other information from staff, you don't want board members to ever feel like you're keeping information from them or hiding problems.

161. Use board members' skills appropriately.
A successful board recruits people with specific skills the association needs to move forward. But once those board members sign on, they must be allowed to actually use those skills. Otherwise, they will become disenchanted or disconnected.

162. Plan in partnership.
Use the annual strategic planning retreat as another tool for defining and clarifying roles and responsibilities of staff and board. Working together on the process of planning strategic directions will help the two sides see the best ways to put their skills to work for the good of the association.

163. Be equal partners.[13]
The board cannot operate effectively without staff support and guidance. The staff cannot operate without the board's strategic vision. Which group is most important? Well, neither.

164. Make sure the chair gets the support and any coaching needed to fulfill his or her role.
A chair needs to have leadership ability, effective listening skills, and a stomach for tough issues, including disputes involving board members. Consider ways to position your board chair for an effective term of service by providing the information, resources, and support he or she will need to serve with distinction. Do this before the new chair assumes office if at all possible.

---

[13] Ideas 161–163 reprinted with permission from "Drawing the Line: Board and Staff" by Jean Block in *Associations Now/The Volunteer Leadership Issue,* January 2006.

Board Relationship Assessment

Here are some key questions you might ask yourself as you evaluate your relationship with your board members and chair:

Clarifying Vision
- How will my chair and I operate this year, and what will success look like in 12 months?
- How have I established the rules of engagement in the past?
- How was this tied to our strategic plan?
- Do I understand what motivates my volunteer leaders and how they would like their work recognized?

Establishing Effective Communication
- Do I understand how best to communicate with my volunteer leaders?
- How do I manage different communication styles?
- How do I avoid pitfalls in communicating with volunteers?
- Do I have a system in place for regular communication with my board?
- What types of information do I think are important to communicate on a regular basis?

Ensuring Effective Training
- Have I invested sufficient time and resources in training my board members?
- What training or orientation program is in place?
- What kinds of training do I need to provide for the entire board versus my new board members?

Determining Roles and Responsibilities
- What have I done to ensure that the roles and responsibilities of the chair are clear and meaningful?
- Are my staff and volunteers clear on who does what, when?
- Have I established a clear chain of command for staff and volunteers to follow?

continued on next page

continued from previous page

Understanding Performance Expectations
- Do I have a good understanding of my board's expectations and how my performance will be evaluated?
- What specific goals did the board and I agree upon?
- How (and when) are they being measured and discussed?
- What relevant information should I communicate to the board relative to my performance, and how should I communicate it?

Reprinted from "Staying on Board" by Apryl Motley, CAE, *Association Management*, March 2005.

165. Facilitate timely follow-up concerning minimum commitments.

The board chair (or another board member designated as the enforcer) should act immediately to inform board members when their participation is becoming unacceptable. Calling a member who has missed successive meetings and is subject to removal is a professional and appropriate form of intervention. Determine whether absences are due to unavoidable schedule conflicts, the member's discomfort with discord between board factions, or other issues.

166. Never forget board members after they become involved.

Continually offer assistance in a positive fashion and communicate with them on a regular basis. Provide regular communication about additional or new opportunities matching their areas of interest and expertise.

167. Maintain an open-door policy for discussion and assistance, at any time.

Offer an opportunity for confidential discussion, if needed.

168. Be organized.

As staff assists board members, always take the "how-can-I-help" approach. Offer organized and professional staff assistance to help them be successful. Have policy manuals, bylaws, and other reference documents readily at hand during offsite meetings.

169. Plan for effective transitions.
A successful association leadership transition maps the landscape, prepares for contingencies, and minimizes the need for decision-making. Simultaneously, an association needs to enable an orderly transition of its elected officers to ensure continuity, and to achieve its strategic budgeted goals. When the incoming leader works with the outgoing leaders for the year before taking office, a successful transition becomes a seamless, productive, and unifying experience.

170. Establish and maintain appropriate boundaries.
Both staff and board members should be clear on their respective roles, how they should communicate with each other, and who has authority to act on behalf of the association in specific situations. (See sidebar "Boundary Statements.")

Boundary Statements

Staff reports should be fully reflective of what has occurred and what expectations have not been met. Information should flow freely between board members and staff; however, staff members shall not seek a decision from or the execution of influence by any board member. Board members shall not condone staff approaches to board members unless it is to report illegal or grossly unethical activity.

With the exception of the president acting on behalf of the board, board officers acting within their authority as set forth in the bylaws, or individual board members acting pursuant to specific authority delegated to them by the board as a whole, no individual board member may direct the executive director or any other staff member.

The executive director shall have the authority, within such operational policy limits as the board may from time to time enact, to pursue the organization's ends as set forth in its mission statement and strategic plan.

Source: National Association of Housing Co-ops.

171. Make sure each party in the relationship understands its own responsibilities and those that fall in the other's purview.

The way in which the board and staff conduct their business needs to reflect this understanding. Clear expectations for the board and the chief staff executive need to be established and maintained because a board that is overly active in management can inhibit the organization's effectiveness.

172. Establish a regular meeting for the board chair and the chief staff executive.

Although the chief staff executive is hired by the full board, it isn't feasible or productive to have the entire board manage that person. It is the responsibility of the chair to supervise the lead staff person. These two people need to meet regularly, not just thirty minutes before a meeting or when a crisis arises.

173. Develop a clear definition of the board's role collectively.

Is it to raise money? Increase profile? Create policy? This leads to the type of individuals you choose. If this is not clear, board and staff often come on with very different assumptions about their jobs, which can lead to misunderstanding and conflict.

ENHANCING THE BOARD MEMBER'S EXPERIENCE

174. Reiterate the benefits of being a board member.
Serving on a board of directors is beneficial to your members in a number ways, including increased visibility and credibility, the opportunity to build their personal networks, and participation in valuable training.

175. Recognize their contributions.
Recognition need not be elaborate or expensive but should be appropriate and presented with sincerity. Recognition may be as simple as providing a special ribbon for all volunteer leaders to wear at the convention. Or, it might entail arranging upgraded accommodations or special in-room amenities for those who travel to association meetings. One association might provide volunteers with desk items (mugs, letter openers, and so forth) carrying its logo, while another might host a thank-you reception and give engraved plaques to volunteers.

176. Highlight their professional accomplishments.
If one of your board members has been honored or has her/his name in a newspaper article, email this article to the rest of the board.

177. Always thank them publicly for everything they do for the organization.
Saying thank you to board members in front of the peers can go a long way in reinforcing how valuable they are to the organization and solidifying their commitment to serving.

178. Celebrate accomplishments and progress towards goals at every meeting.
Board members should leave meetings feeling like they have made some contribution to moving the organization's goals forward.

179. Define success.
How does your association define success? There has to be agreement about what matters most. Once you have identified categories of success (i.e. financial goals, business operations, learning and growth, and so forth), you will be able to measure it and communicate with board members about it.

180. Give board members substantive work.
Board members' energy and enthusiasm will be greatly enhanced when you offer them genuine opportunities to deal with issues of real strategic importance. Some associations devote a significant amount of board meeting time to discussion of an over-arching "mega question" such as how to improve chapter relations or how to co-opt gatekeepers who may otherwise prevent the association's message or membership value proposition from reaching intended targets.

181. Quantify their efforts.
Collect data, perhaps quarterly, on how many hours were contributed by board members to complete board and committee business. The data can serve as back up on the Form 990 tax return and also demonstrates an active and involved board. In cases where board members perform tasks that would be staff tasks if

association resources were not limited, this data can be translated into staff-equivalents.

182. Feature board members in your publications and on your website.
This is a great way to highlight their contributions to the association and serves as great PR when you're recruiting new board members.

183. Write personal thank you notes or letters.
In a time of too many email messages and texts, a handwritten note can really make a board member feel special and valued. Use the note to celebrate an achievement, to acknowledge the board member's role (i.e., "We couldn't have done it without you."), and to reinforce the achievement's connection to the association's mission, vision, and strategic plan. Some execs use nice blank note cards and keep them handy. One exec used a preprinted postcard with the salutation, "I caught you doing something right," and then filled in lines for the specifics of what and when.

184. Thank the boss.
Someone freed up the member's work time to work on association business. Check with the member first (and ask for a name), and if they are okay with it, send a letter to the board member's boss.

185. Thank the assistant.
An exec will quickly find out if there is an assistant to the board member who helps keep the schedule and reminds the board member of conference calls and meetings. Thank the assistant and copy the member.

186. Thank the family.
After working together for two or three years, an exec may get to know something of a board member's personal life and who at home is supporting the board member's reduction in personal time. How to thank is challenging, but could include inviting spouses to the winter board meeting in a warm place and scheduling time for spouses to be included in board socials. If the board member is going to receive a special award at the annual conference, try to

get the family there to watch, even if it means using one of your complimentary rooms.

187. Adjust your schedule to meet your president's schedule.
Resolve time zone and office hour conflicts in the volunteer's favor. A president on the west coast may want to call your east coast office from the breakfast table. An attorney president or doctor president may need to talk to you at odd hours if they are in court or making hospital rounds all day.

199 ideas
EVALUATING THE BOARD

188. Create a culture of assessment.
Facilitate ongoing evaluation of the board as whole and as individual board members. The method and frequency of evaluation may change from time to time depending upon the kinds of issues you need to address.

189. Mutually agree on what format to use.
When thinking about the type of evaluation process to use, three areas are usually considered: (1) written versus oral, (2) numbers versus commentary, and (3) board evaluation versus peer evaluation.

190. Adopt a self-evaluation policy.
Board policy should include a policy on the board self-evaluation, which may be accompanied by implementing procedures.

191. Focus on self-evaluation as a performance improvement process rather than an annual event.
Rather than focusing only on how an annual self-evaluation should be conducted, board members should consider the more important question of how self-evaluations can be used to improve the performance of the directors, the board and, ultimately, the association itself. From this perspective, the self-evaluation is more than an

isolated annual event. Effective self-evaluations will provide critical information about the composition of the board, the board's relationship with management, and the effective operation of the board and its committees. Board leaders should view annual self-evaluations not as exchange-mandated events, but as dynamic processes that will improve performance.

192. Be considerate of board members' time.
In selecting or developing your assessment tool, balance your need to gather information against how much time people are willing to devote to the process.

193. Don't use the same format year after year.
Board evaluations will and should change somewhat from year to year; priorities may shift depending on the critical issues facing the board. Questions should be relevant to the board's current tasks and should be based on the needs of the board at the particular time when the evaluation is planned. Moreover, questions should be targeted to focus on areas of board performance, not CEO and staff performance, which also are essential exercises, but discrete ones from evaluating the board.

194. Establish ground rules.
Determine whether board members' feedback will be solicited anonymously and in what form it will be shared with the entire board and other stakeholders.

195. Compile and discuss the results of evaluations.
The entire board should review the responses from a self-assessment or other evaluation tool and generate dialogue around what's going well and what could be improved.

196. Involve counsel in the evaluation process.
Information gathered during evaluations is potentially discoverable during litigation. As such, you must exercise due diligence in the preparation of any report summarizing the results of the evaluation process.

197. Document what you did right.
Don't lose sight of what was done well. Did you drop an unused service? Forge a new partnership? Solve a troublesome issue with chapters? You want to remember how to do that again, so write it up. If you collect a few years' worth of these positives, you will have a treasury of "how to's" to give to new board members.

198. Ask departing members to reflect on their service to the board.
Their feedback will be useful and could be solicited using a questionnaire (see sidebar "Questions for Departing Board Members").

Questions for Departing Board Members

1. What did you enjoy most about your [ASSOCIATION] board service? What did you enjoy least? What could have been done to make your experience better or more enjoyable?

2. Now that you have completed your term on the [ASSOCIATION] board of directors, what are the three most valuable lessons you have learned about [ASSOCIATION]?

3. What are the three most valuable lessons you have learned about governance matters?

4. What are the primary attributes that made board meetings successful?

5. What are the primary attributes about board meetings that need improvement?

6. Did you feel that your time was spent on important or valuable issues and tasks? Did you feel that you were able to make a difference and that your opinions and contributions were heard and valued?

7. What are the most important issues of consequence that the board addressed during your term of office? Were there issues the board addressed that you think did not belong on the board agenda?

continued on next page

continued from previous page

8. What issues do you think were handled most successfully by the board during your term? What issues could have been handled better?
9. Do you feel as though you had the information and training necessary to be an effective board member and to make decisions at board meetings? If not, how can [ASSOCIATION] improve in this area?
10. How would you characterize the role of the board in governance matters? In operational matters?
11. How do you see the balance of the board's role in policy-making with the staff role in policy-making? The balance with regard to operations?
12. Does a three-year term provide enough time to develop your full potential as a board member?
13. Do you believe that [ASSOCIATION]'s process for selection of board members and board officers is an appropriate one? Is it one that provides for adequate leadership development and succession? Do you have any suggestions for improvement?
14. Did your time on the board help with your own professional development? How?
15. Based on your experience, what advice about board service would you give to a new member of the board?
16. What other issues would you like to comment on?

Adapted from "Questions for Departing Board Members" by Kathleen Curry Santora, *Executive Update: Electronic Issue,* March 2002.

199. Consider using an online evaluation.

Numerous vendors provide this service to boards. Depending on your circumstances an online board self-assessment might be the appropriate tool to help your board standardize and automate its evaluation process.

BIBLIOGRAPHY

Athitakis, Mark. "Better Board Behavior." *Associations Now,* April 2010.

Axelrod, Nancy. *Governing For Growth: Using 7 Measures of Success to Strengthen Board Dialogue and Decision Making.* ASAE, 2009.

Axelrod, Nancy. *Governing for Growth Facilitator's Guide,* ASAE, 2010.

Batarla, Rob. "How to Turn a Financially Clueless Board Member Into a Financial Whiz." *Associations Now,* March 2009.

Block, Jean. "Drawing the Line: Board and Staff." *Associations Now/The Volunteer Leadership Issue,* January 2006.

BoardSource. "The Consent Agenda: A Tool for Improving Governance." 2006.

Burton, Eric. Board-staff Collaboration: Factors for Success. McGill University, Montreal, Canada, 2002.

Carver, John. "Reinventing Governance," *Association Management,* August 1999.

Eadie, Doug. *High-Impact Governing in a Nutshell: 17 Questions That Board Members and CEOs Frequently Ask.* ASAE, 2003.

Eadie, Doug. "The Board-Savvy CEO." in Meeting the Governing Challenge, *Governance Edge,* 2007.

Ernstthal, Henry. *Principles of Association Management.* ASAE, 1988.

Ford, Jane. "Board Relations: Avoid These Mistakes for Better Board and Staff Relationships." <http://EzineArticles.com/?expert=Jane_Ford>.

Frels, Mark. "Motivating Volunteers." *Associations Now,* November 2006.

Furr, Richard and Lana. "Your Board: Proactive Partnering or Reactive Interference?" LeaderValues, 2005. <www.leader-values.com/Content/detail.asp?ContentDetailID=896>.

Gammel, C. David. "Engaging Volunteer Leaders in Web Projects: 5 Keys to Success." *Executive IdeaLink*, February 2010.

Harris, Robert. "Effective Board Orientation." The Nonprofit Center, 2007. www.nonprofitcenter.com.

Harris, Robert. "Minutes Are to Protect the Organization." The Nonprofit Center, 2007. www.nonprofitcenter.com.

Herman, Melanie Lockwood. "Enforcing Board Member Responsibilities." *Associations Now*, November 2010.

Hindman, Sanchez. "Board Meetings: Tips for Becoming More Productive." *Community E-ssentials*, November 2007.

Holler, Harold J. "Let's Meet Virtually, That Is." *Associations Now/The Volunteer Leadership Issue*, February 2010.

Hurley, Gerard. "Ten Documents No Board Should Be Without." *Association Management*, January 2000.

Jacobs, Jerald A. "Board Member Legal Responsibilities." *Associations Now/ The Volunteer Leadership Issue*, January 2010.

Knecht, Pamela R. "Engaging the Board in Strategic Planning: Rationale, Tools, and Techniques." San Diego: The Governance Institute, Summer 2007.

Male, Richard. "Rich Tips." Richard Male and Associates, Denver.

Martinelli, Frank. "Developing a Board Recruitment Plan." The Center for Public Skills Training. <www.createthefuture.com/developing>.

Masaoka, Jan. "Ten Quick Ways to Improve Board Meetings." *Board Café*, CompassPoint Nonprofit Services, 2004.

McNamara, Carter. "Guidelines for Recruiting New Board Members." Authenticity Consulting, LLC. <www.managementhelp.org/boards/recruit.htm>.

Motley, Apryl. "Staying on Board." *Association Management*, March 2005.

Novick, Lou. "Board Orientation: Pointers for a Successful Transition." *Dollars & Cents*, September 2000.

Ohio College Access Network. "Relationship between the Board of Directors and Executive Director." <www.ohiocan.org/ocanbb/AllAccess/ItemPage.aspx?groupid=40&id=429>.

Perry, Gail. "12 Ways to Liven Up Your Board Meetings—and Your Board." *Executive IdeaLink*, February 2010.

Porto, Kim and Janet G. McCallen (with a commentary by Jeffrey Cufaude), "The Café Model: Engaging Associations in Meaningful Conversation." *Journal of Association Leadership*, Fall 2004.

Redding, Whitney. "The Right Metrics for Association Boards." *Associations Now/Volunteer Leadership Issue*, January 2010.

Schlegel, John F. *Enhancing Committee Effectiveness* (revised edition). ASAE, 2009.

Sentry Management Inc. "What Is a Board Member's Fiduciary Responsibility and What Does it Mean?" Newsletter, November 2010. <www.sentrymgt.com/newsletters/what-board-members-fiduciary-responsibility-and-what-does-it-mean>.

Stein, Jeffrey M. and Laura Oleck Hewett. "Key Issues in Board Self-Evaluation." The Metropolitan Corporate Counsel, December 2008.

Tecker, Glenn H., Meyer, Paul D., Wintz, Leigh, and Crouch, Bud. *The Will to Govern Well, 2nd Edition*. ASAE, 2010.

Thomas, Karen Tucker. "The Power of Dialogue—Connect & Engage."

Truesdell, Mark. "Improving Board Meeting Attendance." *Associations Now*, July 2006.

Walker, Larry. "Building Bonds: Pathways to Better CEO Board Relationships." *BoardBrief*. The Walker Company, n.d.

Wardle, J. Bruce. "Passing the Leadership Gavel." *AMC Connection*, June 2010.

Woehlke, James A. "The Substance of Meeting Minutes." *Associations Now*, February 2006.

Wood, Gale. "Making Meetings Productive and Fun." *Association Management*, January 1998.

SHARE TIPS WITH COLLEAGUES

In our ongoing effort to connect great ideas and great people, we're collecting tips and ideas on a variety of topics that will be reviewed, and *if selected,* will be published in a future publication—a collection of "199" tips on a particular topic. You can choose to be credited as a contributor and if your tip is published be listed in the book as such, or you can choose to remain anonymous. Either way, it's a chance to give back to your profession and help others achieve greater success.

If you have questions about our "199 Ideas" series, please contact the director of book publishing at books@asaecenter.org.

Following is the submission form. We prefer that you visit **www.asaecenter.org/sharemytip** to submit your tip electronically via our website. However, if you prefer, you may copy and submit the form by mail or fax to:

> Attn: Director of Book Publishing
> ASAE: The Center for Association Leadership
> 1575 I Street, NW
> Washington, DC 20005-1103
> Fax: (202) 220-6439

Share My Tip Form

Please select the appropriate category or categories for your tip submission:

Board & Volunteers
- ☐ Board Relations
- ☐ Volunteer Relations
- ☐ Volunteer Recruitment
- ☐ Volunteer Engagement
- ☐ Volunteer Retention/Rewarding

Meetings
- ☐ Sponsorships
- ☐ Connecting Attendees
- ☐ Enhancing Learning Experiences
- ☐ Exhibits
- ☐ Generating Additional Revenue
- ☐ Other: _____

Finance
- ☐ Budgeting
- ☐ Cutting Expenses
- ☐ Other: _____

Benchmarking & Research
- ☐ Increasing Response Rate
- ☐ Other: _____

Membership
- ☐ Recruitment/Retention
- ☐ Communications
- ☐ Engagement
- ☐ Program Benefits
- ☐ Dues Structures
- ☐ Globalization
- ☐ Research
- ☐ Other: _____

Technology
- ☐ Other: _____

Time-Saving Tips
- ☐ Other: _____

Please submit your tip below. Please limit to 500 characters. If you require more than 500 characters, please submit via email directly to books@asaecenter.org with the subject "Tip".

continued on next page...

Share My Tip Form
continued from previous page

Name: _____

Organization: _____

_____

Email: _____

Please indicate whether you would like to remain anonymous or be credited as a tip contributor if your tip is published:

☐ Anonymous

☐ Yes, please list me as a contributor.

By submitting your tip, you represent and warrant that you are the sole author and proprietor of all rights in the work, that the work is original, that the work has not been previously published, that the work does not infringe any personal or property rights of another, that the work does not contain anything libelous or otherwise illegal, and that you have the authority to enter into this agreement and grant of license. You also agree that the work contains no material from other works protected by copyright that have been used without the written consent of the copyright owner and that ASAE: The Center for Association Leadership is under no obligation to publish your tip submission.

You also grant ASAE: The Center for Association Leadership the following rights: (1) to publish the work in all print, digital, and other known or unknown formats; (2) to reprint, make derivative works of, and otherwise reproduce the work in all print, digital, and other known or unknown formats; and (3) to grant limited sub-licenses to others for the right to reprint, make derivative works of, and otherwise reproduce the work in all print, digital, and other known or unknown formats.

Signature _____

Thank you for submitting your tip!